ST. JAMES'S CHURCH, FORDHAM, FROM A SKETCH IN THE POSSESSION OF WM. W. WALDRON, A.B. A.D. 1853.

HUGUENOTS OF WESTCHESTER

AND

PARISH OF FORDHAM.

BY

WILLIAM WATSON WALDRON, A.B.,

SECRETARY OF THE FIRST VESTRY.

"Moreover I will endeavor that ye may be able after my decease to have these things always in remembrance. For we have not followed cunningly devised fables."—2 PETER 1 : 15, 16.

INTRODUCTION BY REV. STEPHEN H. TYNG, JR.,

RECTOR OF CHURCH OF THE MEDIATOR, N. Y.

NEW-YORK:
W. H. KELLEY & BROTHER, PUBLISHERS.

1864.

TO THE

RT. REV. WM. HEATHCOTE DE LANCEY, D.D.,

BISHOP OF WESTERN NEW-YORK,

(OF HUGUENOT DESCENT,)

THIS EPISODE IN CHURCH HISTORY IS RESPECTFULLY INSCRIBED.

INTRODUCTION.

A YOUNG man's ignorance is to be the "introduction" to an elder's wisdom. So the author, my friend and parishioner, wills. It is a task which, both for his sake and the important subject to which he has given his time and thoughts, I cheerfully undertake.

The history of the Huguenots in America has been one of very marked interest. In proportion to their numbers, no class of men have imposed such a debt of gratitude as they upon the literature and culture of this country. Their descendants have been worthy successors of noble fathers. Their decided loyalty in these times of sorrow is a grand testimony to that determined conscientiousness, and espousal of neglected truth which were the chief characteristics of their persecuted ancestors before and after their emigration from France. The deeds of St. Bartholomew's day will stand in the memory of the world so long as God's will is to be vindicated and God's word is to be obeyed. It was the Philippian privilege of these noble in the kingdom "in the behalf of Christ, not only to believe on him, but also to suffer for his sake." And we honor and respect the sons for the valorous deeds of their sires. Had they themselves been deficient in the labors so abundantly in these pages recorded, their fathers' praise had yet been their well-founded pride. If glory be due to those who establish an honorable name, greater merit belongs to those who preserve it untarnished.

The preparation of this book, which I am sure will commend itself to the careful perusal of many whose ancient pedigree it traces, has been an unceasing pleasure to the writer. He has devoted untiring energy to the collation of its materials and has disposed them with a master's hand. In the loneliness of a life without family connections of any degree, (all having preceded him to glory,) like the ewe lamb of Nathan's parable—this book has been to him, "as a daughter!" He has fondly cherished it, and carefully watched, with jealous eye, the acceptance it should gain from the critic's examination. And now it is sent forth to perform an honorable mission. Wherever it is read let the covenant God of our fathers be praised for that grace which was given them and continued to their posterity that they might witness a good confession for His name.

S. H. T., Jr.

New-York City, June 8th, 1864.

PREFACE.

It may naturally be asked, why was the subject of the "*Huguenots of Westchester*" selected as the theme for this "*Sketch*," when there are so many others better calculated to convey instruction and entertainment, and the materials for which would have been more accessible? The reply to the inquiry is, that this subject seems to be naturally presented from the circumstances of the case. New-Rochelle and Fordham, the localities wherein were enacted the transactions adduced, being formerly embraced within the boundaries of the only parish in the county, naturally suggested the idea of including their histories within one publication—the obscurity of the origin, rise, and progress of these parishes ren-

2

dering their histories very difficult of access, and not easy to be presented under one connected relation. The author, being fully cognizant of the events he delineates, was induced to undertake the task, prompted by the same motives as the Apostle when he says: "*Knowing that shortly I must put off this my tabernacle, even as our Lord Jesus Christ hath showed me. Moreover, I will endeavor that ye may be able after my decease to have these things always in remembrance; for we have not followed cunningly devised fables.*" *

We cannot omit to acknowledge the politeness of the Rev. Dr. Verren in presenting his able discourse delivered on the occasion of laying the first stone of the "*Church du Saint Esprit*," in New-York, wherein we found many of the incidents recorded in the *Sketch*. To Bishop De Lancey we also owe some feelings of gratitude for the prompt manner in which he acceded to the request of dedicating to him (*the spiritual representative of the Huguenot Church in America*) the Historic Sketch.

* 2 Peter 1: 14–16.

The letters from General Washington to the De Lancey family were presented, several years ago, by descendants of those persons to whom they were addressed, with the express stipulation that they should be published, with which agreement we complied. Those of our readers who have perused that useful work, (of much research,) "*Bolton's History of the Protestant Episcopal Churches in the County of Westchester*," cannot fail to recognize our indebtedness to its indefatigable author. This could not possibly be avoided any more than two travellers, going over the same road, and undertaking to write an account of the scene, could avoid describing similar objects. For the facts collected concerning the Huguenots who took refuge in Westchester, (a mere episode in ecclesiastical history,) I am indebted, in a great measure, to the kindness of friends from whom I procured documents in manuscript, together with records long since published.

The letters appearing in the narrative were given by a great-granddaughter of Stephen

De Lancey, who was from Caen, in Normandy, and came among the persecuted refugees, some of whose descendants still reside in Fordham. The facts, gleaned from such various sources, are presented without any embellishment or pretension, and with a painful consciousness of deficiency in execution, still trusting that their combination, in one continuous narrative, will be conducive to some good, and will convey more instruction than the scattered and detached medley from which they were gleaned.

Of all the religious professors who have found an asylum in America from persecution for conscience' sake, there are none more deserving of historic memorial than the *Huguenots*, who had ceased, as a political body, to exercise power, and were complled to seek, in foreign lands, that protection denied in their own.

The Pilgrim Fathers had a Governor Bradford, the Quakers had a William Penn, to hand down to posterity, records of their wanderings, but *the Huguenots* had not among them any to assume the pen in their defence, or to preserve their memory from oblivion.

The Waldenses, Albigenses, and Huguenots sent out missionaries throughout Germany, Italy, and France, to propagate the doctrines of *Protestants* who received that celebrated name at the "*Diet of Spires*," on the twenty-fifth of April, 1529, when John Duke of Saxony, George Elector of Brandenburgh, and Philip Landgrave of Hesse, with other princes, entered their "*Protests*" against the errors of Popery, in the following words:

"We entreat you to weigh carefully our wrongs and our motives. If you do not yield our request, we '*Protest*' before God our only Creator, Preserver, and Redeemer, who will, one day, be our Judge, as well as before all men and all creatures, that we, for all our people, neither consent nor adhere, in any manner, to the decree made to deprive us of our Christian liberty in any thing that is contrary to God, to his holy word, to our right conscience, and to the salvation of our souls."

It is asserted that the man who has written

a book has made mankind his debtor throughout all time, even though such belongs to that class which only serves as a stimulus to generate inquiry or suggest an original idea. If such be the case, this mite, cast into the treasury of literature, must claim its reward.

HUGUENOTS OF WESTCHESTER.

"How beautiful on the mountains are the feet of them that bring good tidings, that publish peace; that bring glad tidings of good, that publish salvation: that say unto Zion, 'Thy God reigneth!'"—ISAIAH 52: 7.

BEFORE entering on this *Episode in Church history*, it will not be out of the legitimate course to give some preliminary observations on the Reformed Churches of the middle ages, through which the light of Christianity is transferred to us, whether under the denomination of Waldenses, Albigenses, or Huguenots, by which names they were severally distinguished, though all agreeing in spirit and doctrine. The Waldenses inhabited the north of Italy; they took their name from Peter Waldo, a wealthy merchant of Lyons, in France, who lived in great reputation for his Christian zeal and benevolent acts, and success attended all he undertook. Some books by the "early fathers" fell into the hands of Waldo, which imparted light to his mind, and comfort to his soul: a great desire possessed him to procure a translation of the Bible for general distribution. The Bible in Latin was but of little service except to the learned. It is not certain whether Waldo translated the Scriptures himself, or caused the work to be done by others. When the "*Book*" was completed, he placed it in the hands of his countrymen. Did wealth ever confer a greater benefit? The art of printing was not yet discovered. Written copies had to be prepared, so that a complete edition of the Bible would cost a large sum of money. All honor to the good man who thus gave the word of God to the people of France!

The Albigenses took their name from Albi, a town in the south of France. In the twelfth century they were persecuted by Simon de Montfort, who brought a large army against them. Numbers of them fled to England, where Wycliffe was translating the Bible into

English, thereby shedding a light which shone like a star to the souls of men to guide them to their Saviour. Wycliffe was rector of Lutterworth, in Leicestershire, where are still preserved the carved oak pulpit in which he preached, the table on which he wrote, the chair in which he died, and the velvet vestments in which he officiated. Though Wycliffe never left his native land, his writings were carried into every country in Europe, by which many minds were awakened, and prepared for a full knowledge of the Gospel.

The Huguenots were the next sect that received the light of the Reformation. For the facts concerning that portion of this denomination which took refuge in America, I am, in a great measure, indebted to friends, who have placed within my hands manuscripts and rare volumes from which I gleaned the most important facts related in the following pages. The Huguenots of Westchester is an unvarnished combination of historic facts, given without embellishment or pretension.

About two hundred and fifty years ago,

(A.D. 1577,) there was great joy throughout all the dwellings of France, among the Protestants, when the king (Henry the Fourth) had sent forth a decree, from the city of Nantes, in favor of the persecuted Reformers, placing them on a level with the Roman Catholics.

The "*Tales for Young Protestants*" thus define their position. The Protestants were now at liberty to attend to trade and the care of land. Their peaceful and active habits soon made them well known. No looms made finer silk; French muslin was unsurpassed; no ploughs were more busy in the fields, and no vines were more fruitful than theirs. They soon became the best work-people in the country. And this was as it should be; for the purest faith should always be connected with industry and attention to the duties of life.

"Henry the Good," as the king was called, had been once a Protestant; but he changed his religion to retain an earthly crown. Many mourned that he should have forgotten the example and counsel of a pious mother; still he did not neglect the friends of his early youth. He knew their worth, and did much to serve them. His merciful conduct did not please the Romanists, and one day he was stabbed by Ravaillac, a priest, while riding in his carriage in the city of Paris. The Protestants soon found that his son and successor, Louis the Thirteenth, bore no love to them, and caused them many hardships. He was succeeded by Louis the Fourteenth, who revoked the edict given in the city of Nantes, although it was declared by his grandfather, Henry, that it should be perpetual. When it suited the Romanists, they did not scruple to break all the laws which were favorable to the Protestants, even though enacted under the most solemn oaths and pledges. Sorrow and mourning were now substituted for joy and pleasure in many of the castles and cottages of France. The enemies of the truth had obtained the power they wanted, and they were at liberty to oppress as they pleased. Severe laws were passed, in the hope of rooting out the reformed religion. Heavy fines were laid upon those who did not adorn their houses on saints' days, and heavy blows if they did not kneel when a Romish procession went along the streets. They were not allowed to be doctors, booksellers, printers, or grocers. No apprentice could be taught a trade in their shops. If they were heard to sing hymns in public or private, they were sent to prison; their hymn-book was publicly burned, and the Bible was taken out of their houses. Their places of worship were broken into and destroyed; their ministers were sent out of the land, or shut up in jail. The sick could only be attended by Romish priests; and the bodies of those who died were often dragged from their graves, and left to be devoured by wolves and vultures.

The distress of the Huguenots was at its height when they saw their dear children torn from their arms, and carried away to be brought up as Papists. The joy of watching over them, of hearing their simple little prayers, and of telling them of the love of Christ in dying on the cross for sinners, was no more to be known by them. And theirs was the bitter grief of not knowing whether their beloved ones were faithful to the truth, or had denied it; whether they were suffering torture in a monastery or nunnery, or laid in the quiet grave. Times of trial show who truly love the Lord Jesus Christ. It was so now. Many who were once known as Protestants, forsook the faith of their fathers. Some were gained over with titles and honors, others with promises of reward; many from fear of a dungeon and death; and many were bribed with large sums. The common people were offered a freedom from taxes for two years, besides a gift of money, if they would change their religion within one month. Those who would not turn were to pay double taxes, and a fine of ten pounds — a large sum in those days. The consequence was, that many denied their Lord—some from terror, and others from hope of such a reward as the wicked could give. Happy did those think themselves who could make their escape to other lands, even though they left behind them all their worldly goods.

There were sad sights in those days, and they had hard hearts who did not shed tears at the sufferings of the afflicted Christians who remained faithful in evil times. One scene was witnessed, in a country town, which made many weep. The Protestant pastor was to have his limbs broken upon a wheel—the most painful death that could be devised. His persecutors did not terminate his life at once; they delighted in protracting his sufferings. For two days he was left in the deepest agony on the wheel, in the midst of which he thus addressed those who stood by: "Jesus Christ has satisfied for my sins, and not only for mine, but for the sins of those who shall go to him by faith, as I now do. I cast myself upon the merits and death of Jesus, and cling to him as my Saviour and Redeemer. My dear people, receive my last farewell, and know that I preached to you the pure truths of the Gospel, the only path that leads to heaven."

Among others who were faithful were a gentleman and his wife. Soldiers were sent to their house, who rudely burst open the door, and carried away their goods for sale. They converted their splendid house into stables, and carried their beds to be made into litter for the horses. When the ruin of the house was completed, the family, consisting of the parents and four children, were turned adrift on the road, and orders were issued that no one should offer them food. A friend admitted them to his house, but a party of soldiers drove them thence; and after undergoing various misfortunes, they at last reached England, in which generous land thousands of the refugees found a home. A husband and wife tried to escape, and took different roads to avoid suspicion; the man was overtaken, and sent to prison — the wife reached England. Years rolled away before this exiled couple met again. One afternoon a poor Frenchman on crutches entered a coffee-house in Soho Square, kept by a French refugee. It was the resort of the Huguenots, many of whom had turned their skill to good account in the great British metropolis. He made inquiries about his wife from the host, which led to her discovery. Word was sent to her, and she arrived in town, and the long-separated husband and wife met once more.

The shores of England afforded an asylum to most of the Huguenots, where there were many who sympathized in their afflictions and who threw open their houses to receive them, affording food and raiment. The French established the manufacture of silk at Spital-Fields, in London, also at Canterbury and Coventry.

There were also farmers and mechanics. Even many of the nobility engaged in trade from necessity, not having saved enough from the wreck of their fortunes to supply their wants. Previous to this, the English were obliged to import many of the luxuries of life which are now manufactured at home; among these are the arts of calico-printing, the weaving of silk stockings, crapes, bombazines, gauzes, damasks, cambric, etc. In this way they repaid their adopted countries for their protection, and, to the present day, we gather the fruits of the toils and losses which these exiles suffered when driven from their native land for conscience' sake, by the base and cruel act, "The Revocation of the Edict of Nantes."

Many incidents of romance might be related of persons connected with the persecution of the Huguenots. Among these may be mentioned the "*Nun of Jouarre*," in Normandy — Charlotte de Bourbon — daughter of the Duc de Montpensier, of the royal house of France. Charlotte was born in the sixteenth century, and, agreeably to the custom of those days, she was compelled to take the veil. Her mother was a Protestant, and carefully instructed her child in the reformed faith. Her father brought her to the convent, where her flowing locks were cut off, and she was conducted to her cell. Some years passed away, but the lessons that her mother taught and her childhood's happiness were never obliterated from her mind. News was brought that the Huguenots had risen in arms. All Normandy was roused; the nunnery of Jouarre was attacked, and Charlotte escaped. She could not remain in France. She reached Heidelberg, in Germany. Charlotte was now in a land where she could openly declare her faith, and she renounced for ever the errors of the Church of Rome. Charlotte was, after many vicissitudes, married to William Prince of Orange. All honor to the memory of Charlotte de Bourbon! It is not alone for her conversion to the Protestant faith, and for the sacrifices she made in its cause; but we recognize in her the stock from which is sprung the royal house of England. Her daughter, Louisa, was married to Frederick, Elector Palatine, whose granddaughter Sophia was mother to George the First of England, and great-grandmother of the Duke of Kent, Victoria's father, fourth son of George the Third. When raised by the providence of God to be Princess of Orange, well did she adorn her high position. Meekness, charity, and devotion constituted her ornaments—not the plaiting of hair or the putting on of apparel! But dark shadows often come over the sunniest prospects. A large reward was offered to any who should kill the prince —a Roman enthusiast undertook the deed. It was the Lord's Day. The prince and princess had returned from divine worship: as they entered the palace, a shot was fired, and a ball entered the neck of the prince, who fell into the arms of his attendants. There was great joy in the city of Antwerp, where the event occurred, when the prince and princess went in state to the cathedral to return thanks for the merciful deliverance from assassination. The church-bells rang merrily, flags were suspended at the mast-head of every ship, and sounds of gladness were heard throughout the land. Shortly after this, the health of the princess failed, so great was the shock she had received. She perceived that her days were drawing to a close; but in all her afflictions she knew in whom she trusted. Her whole life had been devoted to the performance of sacred duties; she had passed through many trials and vicissitudes, but ever looking forward to a crown of glory that fadeth not away, she was miraculously sustained to the end of her mortal career to inherit that crown. *Sic transit gloria mundi!*

Spain, the stronghold of Catholicism, had its professors of the reformed faith, among whom was a young lady in Seville—Maria de Bohorques—whose early youth was full of hope and promise, yet was led, by divine grace, to leave the Church of Rome and give up her life for the truth.

On the morning of the twenty-fourth of September, 1559, more than one fatal stake was placed in the great square of the city of Seville. A number of the reformed faith were to be burned that day. Early in the morning the monks came to the young martyr's cell. Feeble in body, but strong in heart, she felt that the Lord was with her. Her looks betrayed no fear: it was to her a day of victory and deliverance. Through the flames she knew she would pass to glory. Other young female Huguenots were to be burned in Seville on the same day. They cheered one another, as they stood ready for death, in singing hymns.

It was customary when the victims were bound to the stake to make one more attempt to lead the prisoners to confess; finding that nothing was gained by their attempts, the pile was lighted and they were consumed. The released spirits passed beyond the reach of their tormentors to inherit immortal crowns.

Time works wonders. Of that part of Europe where the Huguenots were persecuted, a modern traveller thus writes: "No nobler page of Christian purity, zeal, love, and holy martyrdom is to be read in the annals of the Church, than that which records the history of the Protestants, or Huguenots, in the south of France. In this whole region they manifested a fidelity unto death. And here Protestantism still survives. I attended service at the old Inquisition monastery: it had all the ardor of French Protestantism. The young pastor preached earnestly and faithfully, with much grace of manner and pathos of expression, to a flock small but most reverent and attentive, composed, for the most part, of humble people. I was completely overcome when they joined in those peculiarly spiritual and ardent canticles for which French Protestantism is so remarkable. It seemed like the voice of the witnesses in sackcloth—faithful, pleading, and resigned. In that very chapel, no doubt, during the persecution of the Huguenots, bitter denunciations of Protestantism had been often uttered; and, perhaps, where the good pastor now preached and prayed in peace, some of his predecessors had stood as convicted criminals, listening to the exhortations of fanatical and savage intolerance to abjure their heresies or die; for at that period mourning and sorrow were spread throughout all the castles and cottages of France. Seasons of trial are the grand test of those who love the Lord Jesus Christ. Many of those who professed Protestantism deserted the faith of their fathers and joined the party in power; some, induced by titles and honors, gave up their religion, Many, from a dread of imprisonment or death.

joined the prevailing side. In these sad relations we see what afflictions many have endured for the Gospel's sake. Numbers of the Huguenots embarked for America, and introduced the mechanical arts which they practised at home, thereby benefiting their adopted country; among whom were the ancestors of those who settled in Westchester County, where they founded a village, which they named '*New-Rochelle*,' after their stronghold in France. Rochelle was the last to submit to the tyrant's yoke."

The city of Rochelle is situated in the department of Lower Charente, on the Atlantic Ocean, and is celebrated in French history for its defence in favor of the Huguenots when the Roman Catholics, under Richelieu, in 1627, besieged it. Being at length reduced by famine, and the loss of fifteen thousand lives, they capitulated, and, escaping from France, they sought asylum in every Protestant country in Europe. Many crossed the Atlantic, among whom were the few that settled in Westchester County, where they built the town which they named after the last stronghold in their native land. Among the Huguenot families who settled here was that of De Lancey, whose ancestor, Etienne or Stephen De Lancey, came from Caen, in Normandy, and some of his descendants still hold valuable possessions in the county, among whom is the present Bishop of Western New-York, to whom this little work is legitimately inscribed.

The Huguenots' first care was to appropriate a portion of their possessions for the support of a minister, for which purpose one hundred acres of glebe was attached to the small frame church they erected. Not satisfied with such an humble structure, they resolved to build one of stone; and so zealous were the parishioners for the promotion of the good work that even the female portion of the congregation repaired to the undertaking, and carried mortar in their aprons to their sons and husbands.

Men of stern and religious principles, they soon erected a church that did credit to their sincerity; it was situated in the rear of the Mansion House, and was opened for divine worship A.D. 1692. The services were conducted according to the Reformed Protestant Church of France.

In 1709, the New-Rochelle congregation, following the example of some of their reformed brethren in Europe, conformed to the Church of England, and agreed to adopt her "*Liturgy and Rites*," as by law established.

Among the families then worshipping here we meet the following familiar names: Bleecker, Lispenard, Guion, Bertain, Le Conté, Nicolle, Angevine, Gallaudet, and Barteau.

The Rev. David Bonrepos, D.D., who had accompanied the refugees in their exile, was appointed first pastor. He preached to the Huguenots in Staten Island, and may be considered the earliest French missionary.

The Rev. Daniel Boudet was the second minister of the church of New-Rochelle.

Colonel Heathcote thus describes this zealous clergyman: "He is a good man, and preaches very intelligibly in English, which language he uses every third Sabbath, when he avails himself of the Liturgy; he has done a great deal of service since his arrival in this country. His pay is only thirty pounds per annum." In the year 1714, M. Boudet took the spiritual charge of the Mohegans, or River Indians. In his reports he states that there were fifty communicants in his church, and he asks for an English Bible and some Books of Common Prayer. After laboring here twenty-seven years, he died in the sixty-ninth year of his age, A.D. 1722.

The third minister in New-Rochelle was the Rev. Pierre Stouppe, A.M. He gives some interesting information in a letter dated December eleventh, 1727, concerning the early settlement of New-Rochelle. He writes: "The present number of inhabitants is about four hundred; there is one dozen houses round the church, near each other, which gives the place the appearance of a town. There are several French families settled within bounds of the settlement, who worship with the congregation. Such was the commencement of the beautiful and picturesque village of New-Rochelle. More than a century and a half have passed away since its founders immigrated to America, and their noble and holy principles have left good influences, evidently discernible in the refinement, morals, and religion of their descendants, still bearing their patronymics. Let it never be forgotten that the Bible came with these early settlers, and was the foundation of their legislation. The Dutch and Lutheran families generally unite with the church when the service is performed in English, and they bring their children to be baptized by the French ministers." There was no school in the place, and the parents supplied the deficiency by instructing their children. There were about one hundred slaves in the settlement, who were taught to read by their mistresses, and were baptized and admitted to the communion.

During the French war (A.D. 1758) great

changes took place in the church; many of the congregation enlisted in the army, and several were removed by death. In July, 1760, the revered and venerable Pierre Stouppe rested from his labors on earth, leaving behind him a reputation unsullied by a stain, after having, for the long period of thirty-seven years, faithfully discharged the duties of his mission. He was greatly respected by his people, and, at the time of his death, the number of his communicants amounted to eighty. As a mark of respect, his remains were interred under the chancel where he had so long officiated. Mr. Stouppe's successor was the Rev. Michael Houdin, A.M., who was the last French preacher in New-Rochelle. This zealous missionary was born in France, in 1705. At the commencement of the war between France and Great Britain, he quitted Canada, where he first settled, and went to New-York, where he read his recantation, being previously a member of the Church of Rome. Having attained great proficiency in the English language, he was invited to Trenton, New-Jersey, to take charge of a congregation, and to labor as a missionary among the Huguenots in that State. When Mr. Houdin and his wife reached New-York, in June, 1744, Governor Clinton, suspicious of all Frenchmen, confined the strangers to their lodgings, and set two sentinels to guard them. His Excellency summoned them before him, when Mr. Houdin first informed him that the French intended to attack Oswego with eight hundred men, being long desirous of possessing that town. After filling the office of missionary for some years, in Jersey, he was employed, in 1759, as a guide to General Wolfe, in his expedition against Quebec. Before he undertook this business, he preached to the Provincial troops destined for Canada, *in St. Peter's Church, Westchester*, from St. Matthew, 10 : 28 : "*Fear not them which kill the body.*" This church, at that time, was the only parochial place of worship in a district of many miles, including Fordham, New-Rochelle, West-Farms, etc. The chaplain escaped the danger of the war; but the gallant Wolfe fell, mortally wounded, at the moment of victory, on the Heights of Abraham, September thirteenth, 1759. After the reduction of Quebec, he asked permission to return to his mission again, but General Murray would not consent, as there was no other person who could be relied on, for intelligence, concerning the French movements. When Mr. Houdin returned to New-York, he was appointed "itinerant missionary" to New-Rochelle, by the "Venerable Society" in England, in consequence of his being capable of transacting business equally well in French and English.

Mr. Houdin, returning to New-York in 1761, was appointed to the mission at New-Rochelle, which village, as well as Fordham, was considered within the spiritual jurisdiction of Westchester Village, then the only parish in the county. The French church was named "*Trinity*," and received, at this time, a charter from George the Third, which document the present corporation enjoys with all its trusts and powers. The charter is dated

1762. In 1763, the Calvinists used unlawful methods to obtain possession of the glebe lands. These Calvinists were the few Protestant French families who had not conformed to the Church of England, and of whom Mr. Houdin remarks: "Seeing the Calvinists will not agree upon any terms of peace proposed to them, we are in hopes that the strong bleeding of their purses will bring them to an agreement through the meshes of the law." Our missionary continued his pious offices among the people of New-Rochelle until October, 1766, when death relieved him from his labors. He was a man of considerable learning and research, as well as of irreproachable character. He was not excelled in zeal and energy by any of his predecessors in the Huguenot ministry, and was followed to the grave by the regrets of his numerous parishioners. He was interred under the chancel of the old French church, in the same grave with Boudet and Stouppe. Since the removal of the sacred edifice, to make way for the high-road to Boston, the mortal remains of these faithful and pious laborers, in the service of their Master, repose beneath the public way, and not a memorial stone marks the spot where they lie, or commemorates their usefulness, excellence, or piety. Such should not be the case; but some modest monument might be erected to mark the hallowed spot where the first Huguenot preachers were interred. Mr. Houdin's funeral sermon was preached by the Rev. Henry Munro, A.M., of Yonkers, from Hosea, 4 : 12: "Prepare to meet thy God."

From the death of Mr. Houdin until the Revolution, services were performed in French and English by the Rev. Mr. Seabury, rector of the parish. Mr. Seabury was afterward consecrated a bishop, and was the first American that was so dignified.

In a letter, dated October first, 1768, Bishop Seabury writes: "As there is a number of strolling teachers who ramble through the country preaching at private houses for the sake of making proselytes and collecting money, I have thought it best to visit them occasionally, as well to prevent any ill effects that might arise, and also for the sake of a number of well-disposed persons who live there. I shall, however, carefully attend to the caution you give, not to neglect particular care of East and West-Chester."

During the Revolutionary War the French Church was closed, and its congregation scattered. After peace was proclaimed a parish at New-Rochelle was regularly organized under the name of Trinity parish,* and the Royal

* During the ministry of Mr. Bayard, the present Trinity was erected in New-Rochelle. In 1827, he changed the field of his ministry to Geneva, New-York, and thence to Genesee, and during 1830 reörganized St. Clement's, New-York. In 1840 he made a tour through Europe to Syria and the Holy Land for health. After four months' absence, and on his return, he died at sea, September second. In 1827, the Rev. Lawson Carter, A.M., was called to fill the vacant parish, resigning 1839, when the Rev. Thomas W. Coit, D.D., became rector, and, in 1849, the Rev. Richard U. Morgan, D.D., assumed the duties of the parish, who continues the excellent pastor of this time-honored flock. In a recent visit to New-Rochelle, I found the original bell, presented to the French Church *Du St. Esprit*, New-York, by Sir Henry Ashurst, of

Charter granted in 1762 was confirmed by Governor Clinton, in 1793. What was left of the French congregation became Episcopalians, and from 1781 to 1786 the Rev. Andrew Fowler officiated as rector of the new parish; he was ordained by Bishop Provost. Rev. Mr. Bartow, the first minister of St. Peter's, Westchester, who labored here for thirty years, sleeps in the cemetery of Trinity, not far from the old French Church. Since the organization of Trinity Parish the following ministers have been rectors: Rev. Andrew Fowler, Rev. Mr. Bartow, Rev. Renaud Kearney

London. It *now* calls the people to the Lord's house, as it did more than a century ago in our city. It bears this legend:

"SAMUEL NEWTON MADE ME, 1706."

The Communion plate, a large silver chalice and paten, was the gift of "Good Queen Anne."

There are many descendants of the Huguenots in New-Rochelle, and such children should venerate and imitate the piety of their ancestors, who were providentially led, like Moses and the Israelites, from oppression and bondage to the land of deliverance—the Canaan in this Western world!

The Clove, 1863.

A.M., Rev. Lewis Pintard Bayard, A.M. He was of Huguenot descent, and removed to New-York, where he was rector of St. Clement's. He went to the Holy Land for his health, and was returning to America, but never reached it. He died on the passage, and was succeeded by the Rev. Dr. Coit; he removed to Hartford, and the Rev. Thomas W. Coit, D. D., was succeeded by the Rev. Richard U. Morgan, D. D., the present incumbent.

Previous to the erection of their church in New-Rochelle, these exiles used to attend worship in New-York, a distance of eighteen miles, travelling afoot, along roads scarcely passable; this would not be credible were it not well authenticated by contemporary history: this fact is attested to by the celebrated Huguenot, John Pintard, LL.D., the founder of the Historical Society, who thus writes in his *Recollections:* "The holy sacrament was administered to the Huguenots, at New-Rochelle, four times a year, namely, Christmas, Easter, Whitsuntide, and the middle of September. During the intermissions that occurred, the communicants walked to New-York for that purpose. Prior to their departure on Sunday, they always collected the young children, and left them in the care of friends, while they set off early in the morning, and walked to the city barefooted, carrying their shoes and stockings in their hands; they were accustomed to stop at a rock, about twelve miles from the city, to rest and take refreshments, where they put on their shoes and pursued their journey, and arrived at the French Church in time for service. The earliest French Church in New-York was in Marketfield street, near the Battery. It was a very humble edifice, but still, being the house of God, sufficient to attract the worshippers from Staten Island and New-Rochelle on the Sabbath, where they used to chant *Marot's hymns*—those animating strains that had so often cheered their pious fathers at the stake in the time of the bloody persecutions of their fatherland. With these hymns in their heads, and the little Testaments which they brought from France, concealed in their hair, they enjoyed that peace of mind which passeth knowledge, unknown to their persecutors."

The next place of worship occupied by the Huguenots, was in Pine street. Pressed by the encroachments of commerce, they sold the ground, and built a handsome church in Franklin street, which has passed away to other hands, and they now worship in L'Eglise du Saint Esprit, in Twenty-second street—a building every way commensurate with the advance in arts and civilization. The present rector is the Rev. Dr. Verren.

In the year 1685, the Rev. Mr. Neau, with his wife and daughter, left France for America, accompanied by other Huguenots. The Rev. Mr. Vesey, the first rector of Trinity Church, in New-York, appointed Mr. Neau his catechist, which office he filled for several years, and he might be considered the founder of Trinity School—an institution distinguished among the noble charities of our city. This excellent man closed his profitable life in 1722, and was buried near the northern porch of old Trinity, where he had long worshipped and served. A granddaughter of his married the brave Captain Oliver H. Perry, who was ever ready to defend his country, and their only daughter, Elizabeth Mason Perry, married the Rev. Francis Vinton, D.D., of Trinity Church.

The year 1686 brought a great influx of French emigration. Many Huguenot families who had taken refuge in the Islands of St. Christopher and Martinique, transferred their residence to New-York; among these was Johannes De la Montaigne, who was appointed a member of the Privy Council by Governor Kieft. He purchased a farm, at Harlem, of two hundred acres, for seven hundred and twenty dollars; it was situated on the Eighth avenue, between Ninety-third street and Harlem river. So happy did he feel in this new home, that he called it "*Vredendal*," or *Valley of Peace*. Numerous descendants of this worthy Huguenot emigrant are residing among us, but some have adopted abbreviated names.

What a striking exemplification of humility, zeal, and devotion, do we witness in these exiles from their friends and country, for conscience' sake! Peace did not always reign in the Huguenot community, verifiing the words of Christ when he stated: "*I come not to send peace on earth, but a sword.*" Among the ministers who took charge in the French congregation, was the Rev. Louis Rou, of the Protestant French Reformed Church. During his administration, a great excitement occurred, arising from a party question; the merits of the case were as follows: Stephen De Lancey, a wealthy merchant, and among the chief patrons of the church, was dissatisfied with Mr. Rou, and procured his dismissal for his want of zeal, and some innovations which he had introduced to the church discipline. The deposed minister appealed from the decision of the congregation, to Governor Burnet and his council, who sustained the appellant. Both parties published indignant memorials on a dispute which had proceeded so far, that when De Lancey was elected to the Legislative Assembly, the Governor refused to administer to him the oath of office, alleging that he was not a British subject. De Lancey contended that he had left France previous to the revocation of the Edict of Nantes, and had received denizenship, under the great seal of Great Britain, from James the Second, previous to his abdication. De Lancey was proved to be right, and the Assembly sustained his claims against the Governor. Mr. Rou's assistant, the Rev. Mr. Moulinard, took part against his superior. The consistory stated that they had paid Mr. Rou in full of all demands, and could dismiss him when they pleased. Still, the council decided in Mr. Rou's favor, and directed that the ministers who should officiate on the following Sabbath in the church, must proclaim the same decision publicly, after divine service in the forenoon. All these efforts, however, did not produce reconciliation, as Mr. Moulinard was much opposed to the Church of England.

In the rear of the church was the old French

burying-ground, and here repose many of the *Huguenots* till the resurrection at the Archangel's trump on the last day. On the ancient monuments are still legible the following inscriptions: "Voici le corp de Susanna Landrin, ag. de 18." "Voici le corp de Isaac Coutant, ag. 50." "Here lies the body of André Renaud, who departed this life on Friday, ye 2 day of Dec. A.D. 1758, aged 25 years." The baptismal registry does not commence until the year 1724, and, for the information of those curious in the olden times, we copy one entry:

Ce Dimanche 14 Mars, 1724, a eté baptisé sortie service du matin, fils de Thomas Wallis and Madelaine sa femme, le Peter a eté presenté au saint baptême par Denys Woertman et Elizabeth sa femme Panain et Marraine le dit Peter est né le six du dit mois.

THOMAS WALLIS,	PETER STEUPPE,
DENNIS WOERTMAN,	ISAAC QUANTAIN,
ELIZABETH her × mark. WOERTMAN,	Ancien.

The congregation consists (says Mr. Seabury) of about two hundred persons, French and English. The French understand English tolerably well. The greater part would prefer an English to a French minister, except about six old persons, who only understand French.

The harmony of the French colony was much disturbed by reports, carefully circulated, that they were inviting an invasion of New-York by their compatriots in Canada. In order to avoid the odium which must necessarily arise from this scandal, they called a meeting and framed the following address:

To His Excellency Lord Cornbury, Governor of New-York:

We, the undersigned, pray your Excellency to inquire into the report that we were inviting our countrymen to invade this province; the report has been spread throughout the whole State, and proves pernicious to all the *French refugees* in general, and disturbs their peace and quiet, as it obstructs that affection and familiarity which they had formerly enjoyed with the other inhabitants of this province, to their grief and resentment. We pray your Excellency to instruct your printer to publish the result, for the pleasure and vindication of our reputation in this respect. And your Petitioners, as in all duty bound, will ever pray.

STEPHEN DE LANCEY, JOHN AMBOYNEAUX,
THOMAS BAYEUX, ALEXANDER ALLAIRE,
BENJAMIN FANEUIL.

It is much to the credit of the Huguenots in New-Rochelle, that under all difficulties, they attended to the interests of the church. In evidence we give the following document:

TO THE HON. COL. CALEB HEATHCOTE, AND COL. LEWIS MORRIS, ETC., GREETING:

We are informed of your pious design to build a church for the worship and service of God, and use the Liturgy of the Church of England. We grant you a license to erect such church in such part of the town as you think fit; but said church must not exceed thirty feet in breadth, and forty in length. We give you authority to collect such money from all who are disposed to give it. Given under our hand and seal, this second day of August, 1710.

In pursuance of this license, we, the trustees, have agreed to build a church in the town of New-Rochelle, in the county of Westchester, the said church to be forty feet in length and thirty feet in breadth, between the dwelling-houses of Francis Le Conte and Zachary Ansevain, as judging it the most convenient place.

ANDREW NAUDAINE,
CALEB HEATHCOTE,
LEWIS MORRIS.

Having given what we conceive to be the most interesting details connected with the Huguenot settlement in Westchester County, we shall take a retrospective view of these interesting people before they sought an asylum in our land.

Huguenot was the name given to the professors of the Reformed or Calvinistic religion in France. The origin of the name is variously accounted for; some attributing it to a professor or leader of the name of Hugo, while others state that it is derived from the German word, "*Eidgenossen*," (bound together by oath,) which was the same name assumed by the confederate cantons of Switzerland, and which was afterward adopted by those citizens of Geneva who promoted the alliance of that republic with the cantons of Friburg and Bern, in opposition to the partisans of the Duke of Savoy, who were named Mamelucs, that is, slaves. The word "*Eidgenossen*" being introduced into the French language, was corrupted first into "*Eguenots*," and afterward to *Huguenots*, and the latter name they ever retained. When the Reformation began at Geneva, the party which favored it being, in a great measure, that which had supported the Swiss alliance, retained the appellation above mentioned, and as several of the French Reformers came from Geneva, or were connected in some way with Switzerland, the name extended to France, and was applied to the partisans of religious reform during the times of sectarian wars and persecution.

The Roman Catholics used the name of *Huguenot* as a word of reproach against the heretics. The epithet has become obsolete, and has been substituted by that of the "*Reformés*," or the reformed, which is given to the disciples of Calvin, or of the church of Geneva, in contradistinction to that of the Lutherans or Protestants, properly so called. The wars and persecutions of the Huguenots are mentioned in the articles of Bartholomew. In public documents the Huguenots were styled: "*Ceux de la religion pretendue reformée.*" The principles of Luther and Zuinglius had gained an entrance into France during the reign of Francis the First, and shortly before the extinction of the House of Valois, which terminated on the death of Henry the Third, son of Henry the Second and Catherine de Medicis. Protestantism increased rapidly in France; to check which the barbarous massacre of St. Bartholomew was devised by the king. The last three kings of the "*House of Valois*"—Francis the Second, Charles the Ninth, and Henry the Third—dying without issue, the crown of France reverted to the "*House of Bourbon*," the head of which was the King of Navarre, who ascended the throne under the title of Henry the Fourth.

The Massacre of St. Bartholomew took place August twenty-fourth, 1572, at three o'clock in the morning, when the victims—men, women, and children—were sleeping. The most distinguished among the slain of this sanguinary scene was Gaspard de Coligni, Admiral of France, a hero more to be feared after a defeat than many after victory. On the night in question, an assassin entered his room; the Admiral, divining his intention, said: "Young man, respect these gray hairs, and stain them not with blood." Regardless of the appeal, the murderer plunged his sword into Coligni's bosom. The Admiral's son-in-law, Lord Teligni, fell among other nobles. After killing every member of the family, the soldiers went forward on their dreadful purpose.

The following letters were given to the author by the descendants of those to whom they were addressed, for the purpose of publication:

GENERAL WASHINGTON TO MRS. ELIZABETH DE LANCEY.

General Washington returns his compliments to Mrs. De Lancey, and would, with the greatest pleasure, comply with her request, of permitting her and her daughters to return to Westchester, was it consistent with propriety. Mrs. De Lancey must be sensible that any intercourse between the two armies, at this time, by means of persons (even ladies) who come from one to reside near the other, cannot be allowed.

General Mifflin is, at present, in Philadelphia, but daily expected; when he returns, General Washington will make inquiry into the detention of her servant—a matter which he is at present a stranger to. Mrs. De Lancey may be assured that all possible care shall be taken to procure the preservation of her house, grounds, and other property."

Pass from General Washington.

Permission is hereby granted to Mrs. Elizabeth De Lancey, Miss Anne De Lancey, and Mr. Henry Izard, with their servants, to land at Elizabeth Town, and from thence proceed to Mrs. Kennedy's, at Second River; from thence they will be permitted to proceed to New-York.

"Given at Headquarters, in Bergen County, this sixth day of September, 1780."

From General Washington in regard to the Military Depredations on the Property of Mrs. De Lancey.

Headquarters, June 14, 1783.

Sir: I have transmitted to Governor Clinton the letter of Mrs. De Lancey, which you were pleased to inclose to me.

The acts complained of were committed at a time when neither civil nor military government existed in that part of the country, and while measures were concerting for their reëstablishment, under American laws and polity.

These enormities being totally abhorrent to my disposition, as soon as they were made known to me, I communicated to the Governor, who is equally disposed to promote peace and good order.

The Chief-Justice of the State, supported by a regiment of Continental troops, is now administering justice in Westchester County; since his arrival there, I believe no outrages, like what Mrs. De Lancey complains of, have been experienced, and I hope, ere long, that good order and regularity of government will prevail in that distressed part of the country.

I have the honor to be, Sir, your most obedient servant,

GEORGE WASHINGTON.

Among other documents received from the same quarter were two letters which we shall give, though not immediately bearing on the subject. Their publication will not compromise the feelings of any, as all the parties concerned have long since passed away, while any thing respecting them cannot fail to interest. The first, written nearly a century ago, was to Mrs. Elizabeth De Lancey, from her father, the Honorable Cadwallader Colden, Governor of New-York under the British Government, the first American appointed to that high office.

To Mrs. Elizabeth De Lancey.

Spring Hill, June 8, 1772.

My Dear Daughter: I have yours of the nineteenth of last month, and all the preceding since you went to the country. I am better of late than I have been for several months before, otherwise I could not have persuaded myself to write that Major Clark is an oddity; I know not what to call it if he be not a male coquette. I had a very kind letter from Mr. Izard by the packet; but nothing particular in it. Richard Colden was here yesterday; his wife is so delicate that he is unwilling to be absent from her. I believe he saw Mrs. Izard only once; his lodgings were three miles distant from her house. The Governor came here about three weeks since, in the evening, and went away next morning before six. We expect him and his lady this day or to-morrow; he takes every opportunity to show a particular regard for me. I shall not have the pleasure of seeing you or your children this summer; I cannot go to you. Pray continue to write to me by every opportunity; it gives me the greater pleasure to receive yours as I have such an unwillingness to take a pen in my hand. Speak very affectionately for me to all your children.

Shall I have no more the pleasure of a letter from Anne or Betsey, because I do not answer their letters? For this they must excuse me, and not punish me.

Your very affectionate father,

CADWALLADER COLDEN.

MRS. ELIZABETH DE LANCEY, West-Farms.

The other letter in the same packet was addressed to Dr. Cochran, New-Windsor, by General Washington.

[Copy.]

WEST-POINT, August 16, 1779.

DEAR DOCTOR: I have asked Mrs. Cochran and Mrs. Livingston to dine with me to-morrow; but ought I not to apprise them of their fare? As I hate deception, even where the imagination only is concerned, I will. It is needless to premise that my table is large enough to hold the ladies—of this they had ocular proof yesterday. To say how it is usually covered is rather more essential, and this shall be the purport of my letter.

Since our arrival at this happy spot, we have had a ham (sometimes a shoulder) of bacon to grace the head of the table—a piece of roast beef adorns the foot, and a small dish of greens or beans (almost imperceptible) decorates the centre. When the cook has a mind to cut a figure (and this I presume he will attempt to do to-morrow) we have two beef-steak pies or dishes of crabs in addition, and on each side the centre dish, dividing the space and reducing the distance between dish and dish about six feet, which, without them, would be near twelve apart. Of late he has had the surprising luck to discover that apples will make pies, and it is a question if, amidst the violence of his efforts, we do not get one of apples instead of having both of beef. If the ladies can put up with such entertainment, and will submit to partake of it on plates—once tin, but now iron—(not become so by the labor of scouring) I shall be very happy to see them.

I am, dear Dr., your most ob't servant,

GEORGE WASHINGTON.

Thinking that these letters, as being the production of him who was "first in war, first in peace, and first in the hearts of his countrymen," apart from the interest they must excite in the breasts of those who are most likely to be the readers of these pages, would constitute an interesting episode in the memoir of the "*Great Man*," I sent copies of them to Washington Irving, then occupied on his grand work—"*The Life of Washington.*" According to the custom of this celebrated writer (a biographer worthy of the subject) the following reply was sent by the earliest opportunity:

SUNNYSIDE, April 16, 1851.

DEAR SIR: The documents concerning General Washington came safely to hand, and were, some of them, quite new to me. For your kindness in sending them accept my sincere thanks, and believe me, very respectfully, your obliged and obedient servant,

WASHINGTON IRVING.

WILLIAM W. WALDRON, Esq.

We shall add one more to the above letters as coming from a member of a Huguenot race, and connected with the subject.

FROM THE RT. REV. WM. HEATHCOTE DE LANDEY, BISHOP OF WESTERN NEW-YORK.

GENEVA, NOV. 4, 1863.

W. W. WALDRON, ESQ.:

MY DEAR SIR: Your letter has reached me just as I am starting on a tour. I rejoice at the proposed publication, and should not resist the distinction you propose in regard to myself, except that I am a Huguenot of the New-York class, and another of nearer connection with Westchester might be found. My ancestor came from New-York, and married Miss Anne Heathcote, of Heathcote Hill, Westchester County, where afterwards my father lived, and where I was born. But I am hurried away, and must conclude with consent to the inscription, and due acknowledgment for the same.

Yours, W. H. DE LANCEY.

A great part of the manor of Fordham was formerly in possession of the De Lancey family, whose ancient homestead was romantically situated near the Bronx; even this relic of bygone days has not been spared by time, the fell destroyer of all things — a consuming fire laid the old mansion in ashes, and with it a number of the forest trees which surrounded it, and among them "*De Lancey's Ancient Pine*," which, like a Huguenot of old, stood as a landmark, connecting the present with the past. A bard of other days has celebrated this ancient tree, nearly the last remnant of "*Revolutionary Times*," in the following lines:

DE LANCEY'S ANCIENT PINE.

Where gentle Bronx clear winding flows,
  The shadowy banks between,
Where blossomed bell or wilding rose
  Adorns the brightest green:
Memorial of the fallen great,
  The rich and honored line,
Stands high in solitary state,
  De Lancey's ancient Pine.

There once, at early dawn, arrayed,
  The rural sports to lead,
The gallant master of the glade
  Bedecked his eager steed,
And once the lightfoot maiden came,
  In loveliness divine,

To sculpture, with the dearest name,
  De Lancey's ancient Pine.

But now the stranger's foot explores
  De Lancey's wide domain,
And scarce one kindred heart restores
  His memory to the plain;
And just like one, in age alone,
  The last of all his line,
Bends sadly where the waters moan,
  De Lancey's ancient Pine.

O victim of misguided zeal,
  To tell thy former fame!
Who bid the fretted stone reveal
  The numbers of thy name?
Ere brightening up the eastern sky,
  Another morn shall shine,
In equalizing dust shall lie
  De Lancey's ancient Pine.

O greatness! o'er thy final fall
  The feeling heart should mourn,
Nor from De Lancey's ancient hall
  With cold rejoicing turn;
No, no! the satiate traveller stays
  Where eve's calm glories shine,
To weep as tells of other days,
  De Lancey's ancient Pine.

The benefit which has resulted to these manors (Pelham and Fordham) from the establishment of churches, cannot be too highly appreciated. Though the Huguenots have passed away, the seed sown by them, as the grain of mustard-seed, has become a large tree which in time will overspread the land, from which will spring other branches, bringing forth fruits in the season.

I love the Church—the holy Church,
  That o'er our life presides—
The birth, the bridal, and the grave,
  And many an hour besides.
Be mine, through life to live in her,
  And when the Lord shall call,
To die in her—the spouse of Christ,
  The mother of us all.

A. C. Coxe.

Southey, in his *Book of the Church*, thus writes of the Church of the Reformation:

"From the time of the Revolution, the Church of England has preserved both stability and security. It has rescued the British Islands from heathenism, idolatry, and superstition, and has saved them from temporal, as well as spiritual despotism. Slowly and firmly it has been established in America, where each year it is increasing in strength and influence. The Protestant Episcopal Church of the United States of America is still in heart with the mother church. Let its members, while they review the struggles and sacrifices through which their own exalted privileges have been obtained, lift up their thanksgiving to Him who overrules the events of nations, for the welfare and prosperity of the kingdom of Christ."

APPENDIX.

Having concluded my records of the Huguenots of New-Rochelle, I considered the work completed, until gaining further information on the subject, by researches at the Astor Library, I could not feel satisfied without imparting all the additional information gained on the subject by an appendix on which I expect the critic will not exercise his skill, as such an appendage was not bargained for and consequently not subject to strict scrutiny.

The Huguenots or French Protestants suffered persecution in their own country, beyond what would be credible to any but witnesses of their distress. When we consider the virtues of this "glorious band of brothers," we are amazed at their fortitude and courage. To be a Huguenot was sufficient to insure condemnation. Some were slaughtered in cold blood without any legal form of justice. Their final destruction was completed at the dreadful massacre on St. Bartholomew's Day, when it is supposed a hundred thousand perished. The Huguenots may be considered a kindred sect with the Lollards, who derived their name from the practice of singing hymns, (lullen,) as a mother lulls her babe to sleep. The doctrine which they held was the same the Church of England adopted at the Reformation; their founder was John Wycliffe, whom the Protestant world will always regard with gratitude for his translation of the Scriptures into the language of the people. He was summoned to Rome to stand his trial for heresy, but was relieved from his persecutors by the friendly hand of death, being attacked with a paralysis which terminated his existence.

From the doctrines of Wycliffe sprung those of John Huss the Reformer of Bohemia, who perished at the stake; not, however, before he imparted the spirit of his religious zeal to Luther, from whom we derive our Protestant institutions. From such various and apparently incongruous materials sprung the "Huguenots," whose strange appellation has ever been a subject of controversy among the learned, the latest suggestion regarding the derivation of the name being that of the learned Dr. Trench, Archbishop of Dublin, in his work entitled, *The Study of Words*, in which he says: "It can hardly be any other than a corruption of 'Eidgnoton,' low German for Eidgenossen, confederates." What must have been the feelings of that remnant of the Church which reached Westchester when seated beneath their own vines!

New-Rochelle, the final "Rehoboth" or resting-place "to those persecuted for righteousness' sake," is situated on the Boston turnpike road, near Long Island Sound. As already stated, it was named from Rochelle in France, and several distinguished men have received their education here, among whom were General Schuyler and Washington

Irving. The first Protestant place of worship erected was built by the Huguenots, on the same site occupied by Trinity Church. Madame Knight, who published a journal of her trip from New-York to Boston, a hundred and sixty years ago, A.D. 1704, thus describes this village: "On the twenty-second of December we left Kingsbridge, the first day's journey, for New-Rochelle, where we met good entertainment. This is a very pretty place, and the roads are passable. There is a bridge made entirely of one stone, over which a cart may pass with safety. Here are three fine taverns and very good entertainment for travellers!" After undergoing many changes and vicissitudes, the church building was transferred to the Episcopalians, and in 1770 the Rev. Samuel Seabury, rector of Westchester, performed services until the Revolutionary War broke out, during which the church was closed and the congregation scattered. When peace was proclaimed, a new church organization was effected, and Mr. Theodosius Bartow, a member of the Episcopal Church, was appointed lay reader, which duty he performed until he was admitted to deacons' orders by Bishop Prevost, the first bishop of the diocese. A unanimous invitation was given to Mr. Bartow to become rector of the new parish, which he accepted, and on his resignation, another Huguenot descendant was chosen, the Rev. Lewis Pintard Bayard. The church was consecrated by the Right Rev. John Croes, Bishop of New-Jersey. The Cemetery is in the rear of the building, where repose in peace the remains of the persecuted Huguenots. The communion service of plate was presented to the parish of Westchester by Queen Anne, who also gave a Church Bible, a book of homilies, and a cloth for the communion-table. Among the families who settled in Westchester was that of De Lancey.

During the troubles in France, the De Lanceys, who resided at Caen in Normandy, suffered on account of their devotion to the Huguenot cause. In 1681 Stephen De Lancey fled to Holland, and from thence to New-

York, where he became a merchant. By his wife, Anne Van Cortland, he had five sons and two daughters, of whom the eldest of the former, James De Lancey, was Lieutenant-Governor of the province; he married Anne, daughter of the Hon. Caleb Heathcote, Lord of the manor of Scarsdale, and his descendants still possess his large possessions.

The De Lanceys of Mamaroneck are descended from a branch of the ancient and noble house of De Lanci of Normandy.

At the ancient church at Oise is a tombstone bearing the following inscription:

Ici repose
Haute et puissante Dame
MADAME FRANÇOISE de LANCI,
dame des terres et seigneuries
d'Haramont et St. Germaine,
Hereditaire chatelaine
des Domaines de Botluzey, etc.

As New-Rochelle, Pelham, and Fordham, were integral portions of the parish of Westchester, it cannot be considered irrelevant to touch slightly on the history of the original organization. The first rector of Westchester was the Rev. John Bartow; he was appointed by Lord Cornbury, in the year 1702. In a letter written in 1704, Mr. Bartow speaks with thankfulness of having made many proselytes to our holy religion. Colonel Heathcote, in a letter to the Secretary of the Venerable Society, dated from the Manor of Scarsdale, November 9th, 1705, says: "There is not any gentleman whom the Society hath sent over that is clothed with a fairer character than Mr. Bartow of Westchester, for truly he is a very good and sober man, and is extremely well liked by the parishioners."

Having given all the details connected with that small portion of the Reformed Church which settled in Westchester county, it remains now only to state that the Huguenots of New-Rochelle were a portion of a body of fifty thousand French who fled to England after the revocation of the Edict of Nantes, the authenticity of which statement is confirmed in the charter of Trinity Church in that village. As no other opportunity will occur to make the statement, it may not be out of place to mention here that the first principles of the Reformation appeared in France in the provinces of Picardy and Dauphiny, and to the inhabitants of these provinces should be attributed the credit of that great event which we have the happiness to enjoy. Though Luther, by his zeal and energy, might be considered the master-spirit of the age, and well deserving the epithet of "The Great Reformer," still the way was first pointed out by the Huguenots.

All the credit of the Reformation cannot be arrogated by the male members of the Church, as many females distinguished themselves in the great and ever-enduring revival. Ladies of the most exalted rank exhibited their zeal in the promotion of the great work, among whom may be mentioned Jane, Queen of Navarre, and Margaret, Princess of Valois, sister of Francis the First, who dignified their religion by pure and blameless lives in abandoned and dissolute times.

History has preserved "*a tableau vivant*" of the expression given by Queen Elizabeth and the ladies of her court to their grief and indignation at the massacre of St. Bartholomew's Day. Her Majesty, for several days, refused to give audience to La Mothe Fenelon, the French ambassador, and when he was admitted, the Queen and the court were clothed in the deepest mourning. When Fenelon approached Her Majesty, the lords of the council and the other attendants averted their looks as he passed through them, none condescending to offer a salute. When he approached the Queen she said: "How can you justify your master in his odious crime of assassinating his Protestant subjects?"

PARISH OF FORDHAM,

FROM

INCORPORATION OF THE CHURCH TO THE APPOINTMENT OF THE FIRST RECTOR.

BY

WILLIAM WATSON WALDRON, A.B.,

SECRETARY OF THE FIRST VESTRY.

TO

WILLIAM ALEXANDER SMITH, Esq.,

JUNIOR WARDEN IN THE FIRST VESTRY,

THE UNDEVIATING FRIEND OF THE PARISH, THE ORGANIZATION OF WHICH HE SUGGESTED, THESE RECORDS ARE RESPECTFULLY INSCRIBED.

PREFACE.

In presenting the following little work to the public, the author must forego all attempts at display, and satisfy himself simply with a statement of facts and memoranda as they appear in a "Note-Book" kept by him when fulfilling the duties of "Clerk of the Vestry" during the first year of the existence of St. James's Parish. The difficulties attending the inauguration of a new church can only be known to those who have been engaged in a similar task, as such alone can sympathize with the operators. Ten years have now elapsed since the first *Protestant Episcopal Church* was established in the *Manor of Fordham*, and great and many are the changes which have taken place during that period. Several of the founders of the parish have left the vicinity, while the "Last Enemy" has removed others, thereby making sad inroads upon domestic circles.

It may seem irregular to embrace, within one publication, the affairs of St. James's Church, Fordham, and the Huguenots of Trinity Church, New-Rochelle, but when it is considered that these parishes constituted integral parts of St. Peter's, Westchester, then the only parish in the county, the blending of their histories must appear obvious.

Previous to the Revolutionary War, the Rev. Samuel Seabury, D.D., was rector of St. Peter's, Westchester, a parish then of vast extent and considered within the Diocese of London. America during the English rule had no bishops, and the Rector of Westchester had the honor of being the first American who was dignified with the mitre. The Huguenots of New-Rochelle are also entitled to put in a claim to partake in the honor of the Episcopacy, as the present incumbent of the Western Diocese of the State is a descendant of one of the most distinguished of the Huguenot families of the parish, and whose ancestral possessions at Mamaroneck, his native place, still in possession of their descendants, bear ample testimony to respectability.*

The time may arrive when the record of the humblest parish will be of vast importance; when American churches will have become venerable from antiquity, and their early history will be lost in the mazes of time.

The author has no more to say than express his thanks to those friends through whose kindness and encouragement this volume has been brought to light. If the friendship and good-will of those whose favor it is an honor to enjoy be a sufficient recompense for any trouble induced by such an undertaking, the writer has been amply repaid. The mercy of the reviewer is not implored, as the undertaking is considered below criticism; the indulgence of friendship is claimed, as common courtesy may demand such for the legitimate tribute due to so unprofitable a labor.

* Wm. Heathcote De Lancey, D.D.

FORDHAM.

THE Manor of Fordham, which forms one of the three divisions of the town of West-Farms, was originally included within the parish limits of Westchester. The name is of Saxon origin, and compounded of two words, Ford (ford) and Ham, (a mansion.)

In 1656, we find the whole of Fordham, as well as Yonkers, in the possession of Adrian Vander Donck, whose widow, Mary, conveyed them to her brother, Elias Doughty. The latter, in 1666, sold them to Mr. John Archer, of Westchester, who, in 1669, obtained a confirmation thereof from the Indian Sachem Sachareth.

In 1671, Francis, Earl of Lovelace, Governor of the province, and consequently exercising regal power, erected the same into the *Manor of Fordham.*

From the Archers, the manor passed, through the Steenwicks, in 1684, to the Dutch Church, in the city of New-York, for the support and maintenance of their ministers, ordained according to the Church orders of the Netherlands, etc. Through the liberality, however, of Mrs. Margaret Steenwick, three hundred acres were exempted from the conveyance to the Dutch Church, upon which was situated the old manorial residence of the Archers, (they being created Lords of the Manor,) now substituted by a modern mansion, in which a descendant of the original proprietor resides.

The family of Archer is of English origin, and held, for many centuries, large possessions in the county of Warwick. Fulbert L. Archer, the first of whom any thing is known, came into England with *William the Conqueror.* The representative of the senior branch, A.D. 1600, appears to have been John Archer, of Warwickshire. At what period the Archers immigrated to this country is uncertain, but, as early as 1630, occurs the name of Samuel Archer, a freeman of Salem, Massachusetts.

John Archer, the first proprietor, accompanied the early settlers from Fairfield, Connecticut, to Westchester County, in 1654. He died in 1685. John Archer, eldest son of the said proprietor, was elected a *vestryman* for the precinct of Yonkers, in 1703, an official dignity which he held for seven years. Little is known concerning the early history of religion here, except that as early as 1671, the inhabitants residing between the two kills of Harlem and the Bronx, were obliged to contribute toward the support of a minister of religion. In 1696, a society was organized here by the Collegiate Reformed Dutch Congregation of New-York, over which the Rev. John Montaigne was appointed minister. Colonel Lewis Morris, writing to the Propagation Society of London, in 1709, says: "I have used my endeavors to persuade the Dutch in my neighborhood into a good opinion of the Church of England, and have had that success that they would, I believe, join the Church in the sacraments and other rites, had they the Dutch Common Prayer-Book, and a minister who understood their language. I have taken some pains with one of their ministers, Henricus Beyse, and have prevailed on him to accept '*Episcopal Ordination.*'"

The old Dutch meeting-house, erected in 1706, which has long since been destroyed, stood on the farm of Mr. James Valentine. Its last minister, previous to the Revolution, was the Rev. Peter Tetard. The following inscription is taken from a stone which formed part of the foundation of this building: I. V. S., 1706.

The Dutch, who constituted a large majority of the inhabitants of Fordham, were not wholly regardless of their spiritual concerns, for shortly after New-York passed from Holland to Great Britain, we find the following petition presented to the Governor in council:

"To the Hon. James De Lancey, His Majesty's Lieutenant-Governor and Commander-in-Chief over the Province of New-York and the Territories depending thereon in America, in Council. That your Petitioners, intending to apply to the General Assembly of this Province for leave to bring a bill into that Honorable House, to enable them to sell and dispose of those lands known by the name of the *Manor of Fordham*, in the *County of Westchester*, either altogether or in parcels, as they shall judge best, to and for the use and benefit of their said Church, did (pursuant to His Majesty's Royal Instructions, relating to the passing of private Bills in this Province) cause an advertisement to be affixed to the door of the Parish Church, in Westchester, declaring their said intentions, where the same remained upward of four weeks successively. Your Petitioners, therefore, humbly pray to make proof to your Honor, that the said advertisement was affixed to the Parish Church, and that you will grant a certificate thereof, and your Petitioners, as in duty bound, will ever pray."

NOTICE.

This is to certify that due canonical notice of the formation of a new church and parish in Fordham, Westchester County, New-York, to be known as St. James's Church, in the manor of Fordham, town of West-Farms, County of Westchester, was given at the time of divine service, at Grace Church, West-Farms, on the morning of Sunday, July seventeenth, and also on the morning of Sunday, July twenty-fourth, both in the year 1853.

WASHINGTON RODMAN,
Rector of Grace Church,
West-Farms.

There being no Protestant Episcopal Church in the Manor of Fordham, where reside many members of that denomination of Christians, who experience much inconvenience on account of having no place of worship within some miles of them, and considering, moreover, in the great increase of the population, that the cause of the Church might suffer by having no spiritual provision made for her members, where those of other sects are so amply provided for, a meeting was called, which assembled at the house of William Alexander Smith, Esq., on the fifth of July, 1853, for the purpose of organizing a parish, and adopting such measures as would most effectually conduce to the same. Oswald Cammann, Esq., was unanimously invited to take the chair, and William Watson Waldron was requested to act as Secretary. The meeting then proceeded to business, when the following resolutions were adopted:

Resolved, That the persons present do proceed to incorporate themselves into a religious society, in communion with the Protestant Episcopal Church, in the United States of America, and that said church and congregation be known in law by the name, style, and title of the *Rector, Wardens, and Vestrymen* of St. James's Church, in the Manor of Fordham, town of West-Farms, and County of Westchester.

Resolved, That the meeting do now proceed to choose two Wardens and eight Vestrymen.

The latter resolution being duly acted upon, the following persons were elected

Church Wardens.

LEWIS G. MORRIS,
WILLIAM ALEXANDER SMITH.

Vestrymen.

OSWALD CAMMANN,
FRANCIS McFARLAN,
WILLIAM WATSON WALDRON,
GEORGE BEMENT BUTLER,
SAMUEL RAYMOND TROWBRIDGE,
GULIAN LUDLOW DASHWOOD,
WILLIAM OGDEN GILES,
NATHANIEL PLATT BAILEY.

Resolved, That the elections for Wardens and Vestrymen shall hereafter take place annually, on Monday of Easter Week.

Resolved, That the Secretary be requested to notify the members of the Vestry (not present) of their election.

The church being now organized, Mr. Cammann left the chair, and Mr. Smith was called thereto, when the thanks of the meeting were voted to Mr. Cammann, previous to adjournment.

CERTIFICATE OF INCORPORATION.

To all these presents may concern:

We, whose names and seals are affixed to this instrument, do hereby certify that on the twenty-sixth day of July, in the year of our Lord one thousand eight hundred and fifty-three, the male persons of full age belonging to churches and congregations worshipping in the town of West-Farms, at places in which divine worship is celebrated, according to the rites of the Protestant Episcopal Church, in the State of New-York, assembled at the house of William Alexander Smith, Esq., in Fordham, pursuant to notice duly given at the time of morning service, on two Sundays previous thereto, for the purpose of incorporating themselves, and of electing two Church Wardens and eight Vestrymen; and we further testify that Oswald Cammann was, by a majority of the persons so assembled, called to the chair, and he presided at said meeting. Lewis G. Morris and William Alexander Smith were duly elected Church Wardens of said congregation and church, and Oswald Cammann, Francis McFarlan, William Watson Waldron, George Bement Butler, Samuel Raymond Trowbridge, Gulian Ludlow Dashwood, William Ogden Giles, and Nathaniel Platt Bailey were elected Vestrymen. That Monday in Easter Week was, by said meeting, determined and declared as the day on which the said offices of Church Wardens and Vestrymen should annually, hereafter, be vacated, and successors be chosen to fill the vacant places, and the said meeting determined that this congregation and church should be known, in law, by the name, style, and title of the "*Rector, Wardens, and Vestrymen*" of St. James's Church, in the Manor of Fordham, town of West-Farms, County of Westchester.

In testimony whereof, We, the said Oswald Cammann, who presided, Wm. Alexander Smith, who was present, and Wm. Watson

Waldron, the Secretary of the meeting, the witnesses of the proceedings aforesaid, have hereunto subscribed our names and affixed our seals this twenty-sixth day of July, in the year of our Lord one thousand eight hundred and fifty-three.

Oswald Cammann,
Wm. Alexander Smith,
Wm. Watson Waldron.

Benefactions to the Parish.

Surplice, Bible and Prayer-Book, Miss Ogden; Baptismal font and lectern, Rev. Mr. Weaver; Gothic chairs for chancel, Wm. C. Maitland; stained-glass windows, Misses Cammann and J. Morris; library of two hundred volumes, Wm. W. Waldron, A.B.; Communion-service, Ladies of the Parish; two hundred dollars and books, Mrs. Alexander Brown.*

* Mother of Sir William R. Brown, Bart.

Sunday-School.

A LARGE Sunday-school was soon in operation, which was attended by a hundred children, and an efficient corps of teachers of both sexes. We consider the institution of Sabbath instruction as being one of the most distinguished feature of the times, and conducing as much to the cause of religion as the Church itself, inasmuch as it commences its work when the plant is tender, in compliance with the advice of the wise man: "Train up a child in the way he should go, and when he is old he will not depart from it."

We have now given a short account of the organization of the *first Protestant Episcopal Parish* in the Manor of Fordham, and however great the difficulties attending the undertaking, we feel amply repaid when reflecting on the prospective good that must result to the neigborhood from the fruits of the tender plant which has been placed in this part of the Lord's Vineyard:

O Thou, who canst with equal eye
  Regard the fate of all,
A world from its bright orbit fly,
  The lowly sparrow fall;
Thine arm almighty, Lord, extend
  To guard this Church from harm,
The Christian pilgrim to defend,
  Thy saints from false alarm.

Oh! may the plant we humbly rear,
  How slow soe'er it grows,
Yet overspread the desert drear
  And blossom as the rose;
Long may its sov'reign balm impart
  To every soul distrest
A cure to heal the broken heart,
  And to the weary—rest.

The parish being now duly organized, we had to consider how we were to raise a building suitable; this difficulty was in some measure obviated by the vestry hiring the Reformed Dutch place of worship for the Sabbath afternoons, at a specified price. When the short lease had expired for which it was engaged, an offer for renewal was made to the

Presbytery, but rejected. No alternative now remained but to procure some place for worship, and the old district school-house was offered for sale, when the Vestry purchasedit, and subsequently removed it to the lot previously bought for a cemetery and permanent site. It is a wild and romantic spot, still retaining vestiges of the primeval forest, appearing almost indicative of the moral waste formerly overspreading this region, but now, we trust, cleared away never to return. How thankful should we be to the great Head of the Church for enabling us, in our time and generation, to accomplish an undertaking several times attempted in vain! 'Tis true, this "*House of God*" looks humble and lowly amid the stately mansions by which it is surrounded, but we trust the day is not far distant when a temple will be raised, in this parish, for the worship of the Deity, in unison with the spirit of the age, and commensurate with the respectability of the Protestant Episcopal Church in the United States of America. Though long in anticipation of the fact, it does not seem irrelevant to introduce thus early in our history some resolutions passed long subsequent to these events, as no more opportune place may occur for introducing them. At a meeting held to open a subscription-list for St. James's Church, the following Resolutions were passed:

Whereas, The building now used as a place of worship by the congregation of St. James's Church, Fordham, is unsuitable to the wants of said congregation, We, the undersigned, being duly impressed with the important duty of making provision for all who may desire to be connected with said church, do hereby pledge ourselves to pay over to such person or persons as may be appointed by the Vestry of said St. James's Church, the several sums of money set opposite to our names, on the following conditions, namely: This money shall be expended, by said Vestry, in erecting a substantial stone church on the ground now owned by the Corporation of said church, the cost of which building, when completed, shall not be less than ten thousand dollars.

The Vestry shall appoint a Treasurer, who shall give bonds for the true and faithful performance of his duties in receiving and disbursing said money, as they may direct. The money shall be paid so soon as an amount equal to ten thousand dollars has been subscribed. The corner-stone of said church shall be laid, if possible, on or before the first day of July next, and the church erected without unnecessary delay. Here follow the names of the subscribers. Four gentlemen, namely, Messrs. Bailey, Schwab, Camp, and Morris, subscribed a thousand dollars each.

The present church is situated between the parallel roads leading respectively to King's Bridge and the High Bridge, and is directly opposite to the Croton Aqueduct. We considered it necessary to make this digression in order to render more explicit the events we have undertaken to record. All things being arranged for commencing operations, we shall proceed with our history, and accurately narrate a few of the principal events connected with the origin, rise, and progress of "Our Parish," until placed *under* the guardianship of its first Rector.

Sunday, June 11, 1854.

St. James's Church, Fordham, was opened for divine service on Sunday, June eleventh, 1854. The Rev. Washington Rodman, Rector of Grace Church, West-Farms, officiated. This humble edifice, however modest in appearance, enjoys a distinction which can never be possessed by any other temple erected for a similar purpose. It is the *First Protestant Episcopal Church in the Manor of Fordham*, and great and many were the difficulties attending the undertaking. A discourse was preached from the following text: "The kingdom of God suffereth violence, and the violent take it by force." (Matt. 11 : 12.)

Sunday, June 18, 1854.

The Church was not less respectably attended than on the previous Sabbath. On this day the Sunday-school was organized, and there was a good attendance of pupils and teachers. I regard these humble institutions as constituting a remarkable feature of our time, and one for which the rising generation should feel grateful, and show their gratitude by obeying their instructors, who, *without fee or reward*, labor so assiduously "to lead them in the way they should go, that when they are old they may not depart from it!" Mr. Henry J. Cammann, A.B., undertook the superintendence of the school, a duty which he so ably discharged at St. Thomas's Church, New-York. The services were performed by the Rev. Dr. Jackson, Rector of Saint Peter's, Westchester. The text was: "My son, give me thy heart." (Prov. 23 : 26.)

SUNDAY, June 25, 1854.

The heat of the weather was so intense, the congregation was not so large as on the former occasions. Much difficulty was experienced in securing the attendance of efficient ministers to perform the services. The Rev. Mr. Murcher, from Ohio, officiated, and his sermon gave general satisfaction. The text was:

"Be not deceived; God is not mocked: for whatsoever a man soweth, that shall he also reap. For he that soweth to the flesh, shall of the flesh reap corruption; but he that soweth to the spirit, shall of the spirit reap life everlasting." (Gal. 6 : 7, 8.)

Sunday, July 2,1854.

This was the first time, since the opening of the church, that services were performed morning and afternoon. Mr. Murcher officiated at both services. In the morning the congregation was small. At the afternoon service a large number attended. Two good discourses were delivered by the reverend preacher from the following texts:

"The secret things belong unto the Lord our God: but those things which are revealed belong unto us and to our children for ever, that we may do all the words of this law." (Deut. 29 : 29.)

"How long shall thy vain thoughts lodge within thee?" (Jer. 4 : 14.)

Sunday, July 9, 1854.

No regular minister being yet provided, the services were necessarily uncertain. The clergyman to-day not having arrived, Mr. Smith and Mr. Henry J. Cammann volunteered their services in reading the prayers and lessons. The choir were at their post and concluded by singing the following hymn:

Softly now the light of day
Fades upon the sight away:
Free from care, from labor free,
Lord, I would commune with thee.

Thou, whose all-pervading eye
Naught escapes, without, within,
Pardon each infirmity,
Open fault and secret sin.

Soon for me the light of day
Shall for ever pass away,
Then from sin and sorrow free,
Take me, Lord, to dwell with thee.

Thou who, sinless, yet hast known
All of man's infirmity,
Then, from thine eternal throne,
Jesus, look with pitying eye.

Sunday, July 16, 1854.

This afternoon the attendance at church was larger than on any former occasion. The services were performed by the Rev. Mr. Rodman. The text on which he preached was the seventeenth verse of the fourth chapter of Matthew:

"From that time Jesus began to preach, and to say, Repent: for the kingdom of heaven is at hand."

Sunday, July 23, 1854.

This is the seventh Sabbath that divine service has been celebrated in our church, and we have reason to be thankful to Providence for the success that has hitherto attended the undertaking. The officiating minister was the Rev. Erskine M. Rodman, this being the first time since his ordination he was called upon to discharge the duties of his sacred office. His text was:

"What shall we do then?" (Luke 3 : 10.)

Sunday, July 30, 1854.

The same minister officiated to-day as on

the preceding Sabbath. His words were practical and such as to impart satisfaction to all present. The text was:

"What mean ye by this service?" (Exodus 12 : 26.)

Sunday, August 5, 1854.

This being a very pleasant day, the attendance at church was larger than usual. The Rev. Mr. Flagg preached on the necessity of prayer. The text was:

"Pray without ceasing." (1 Thess. 5 : 17.)

Sunday, August 13, 1854.

The Rev. Jesse Pound gave his services today; his sermon was simple and calculated to convey useful instruction. The text was:

"Seeing then that all things shall be dissolved, what manner of persons ought ye to be in all holy conversation and godliness?" (2 Peter 3 : 11.)

Sunday, August 20, 1854.

The Rev. Cadwallader C. Hoffman, the African Missionary, was expected to preach, but being unavoidably detained elsewhere, he sent word that he would officiate in the evening.

At the appointed time there was a good congregation assembled, who seemed much gratified by his discourse. The text was:

"For thus saith the Lord of hosts, Yet once, it is a little while, and I will shake the heavens, and the earth, and the sea, and the dry land; and I will shake all nations, and the desire of all nations shall come: and I will fill this house with glory, saith the Lord of hosts. And the silver is mine, and the gold is mine, saith the Lord of hosts!" (Haggai 2:6, 7, 8.)

Sunday, August 27, 1854.

No minister being yet appointed, we were obliged to have recourse to lay services, and we availed ourselves of the assistance of Mr. Henry J. Cammann, Superintendent of the Sunday-school, as the clergyman we had engaged did not arrive. The volunteer choir closed the sacred ceremonies of the day with the following hymn:

Eternal Source of every joy,
Well may thy praise our lips employ,
While in thy temple we appear
To hail thee Sovereign of the year.

Wide as the wheels of nature roll,
Thy hand supports and guards the whole;
The sun is taught by thee to rise,
And darkness when to veil the skies.

The flowers of spring, at thy command,
Perfume the air and paint the land;
The summer rays with vigor shine,
To raise the corn and cheer the vine.

Sunday, September 3, 1854.

The weather being oppressively warm, the congregation was small. The Rev. Mr. Draper, of Harlem, officiated. The discourse was excellent from the following text:

"And I say unto you, Make to yourselves friends of the mammon of unrighteousness; that, when ye fail, they may receive you into everlasting habitations." (Luke 16 : 9.)

Sunday, September 10, 1854.

After a long drought, the windows of heaven were opened and a storm of unusual length and violence was sent to refresh the parched earth. In this state of the weather very few could be expected, and as no clergyman attended, lay services were observed.

Sunday, September 17, 1854.

Beautiful did the earth appear on this bright Sabbath morning, clothed in its rich garments after the refreshing rains so lately sent from heaven. A large congregation assembled to hear the Rev. Benjamin Akerly, who went through the services in his customary efficient manner. The text was:

"But grow in grace, and in the knowledge of our Lord and Saviour Jesus Christ." (2 Peter 3 : 18.)

Sunday, September 24, 1854.

Our church commences, under its own rector, to-day. The Vestry have called the Rev. Joshua Weaver, A.M., to the pastorate, and he gave us an excellent discourse from the following text:

"Let me die the death of the righteous, and let my last end be like his." (Numbers 23 : 10.)

Sunday, October 1, 1854.

This may be considered THE BIRTHDAY of our Church, as we now work under our own rector, and it is the first time that we have enjoyed the full privileges of using the morning and evening services, and the collect of the day seems so appropriate to our circumstances that I shall transcribe it:

"O Lord, we beseech thee, let thy continual pity cleanse and defend the Church; and because it cannot continue in safety without thy succor, preserve it evermore by thy help and goodness, through Jesus Christ our Lord. Amen!"

Mr. Weaver preached from the following text:

"What fruit had ye then in those things whereof ye are now ashamed? for the end of those things is death." (Rom. 6 : 21.)

Afternoon.

The church was again opened at half-past three P.M., and Mr. Weaver gave as his text the following words:

"And this is the will of him that sent me, that every one which seeth the Son, and believeth on him, may have everlasting life:

and I will raise him up at the last day." (John 6 : 40.)

The Rector gave notice that the church building would be removed, during the ensuing week, to its final location, not having been taken from the lot on which it was erected originally.

Sunday, October 8, 1854.

The church building was moved from its site since last Sabbath, but not yet placed on what is to be its permanent destination, which is about a hundred feet from the place where it originally stood. Many persons who came to worship were afraid to enter the building, supposing that the structure was unsafe, in consequence of being so recently moved; these terrorists lost an edifying discourse delivered by the rector from the following text:

"And shall lay thee even with the ground, and thy children within thee; and they shall not lay in thee one stone upon another; because thou knewest not the time of thy visitation." (Luke 19 : 44.)

Sunday Afternoon.

Service commenced at half-past three o'clock. The text was:

"For your fellowship in the Gospel from the first day until now." (Philippians 1 : 5.)

Sunday, October 15, 1854.

In consequence of a severe storm, our "*Tent in the Wilderness*" had not arrived home. Still there was little doubt but that the next Sabbath would find her domiciled in her last resting-place, when we shall close this record of current events, as we trust all circumstances connected with the church and parish are preserved in the minutes of the Vestry. The Rector preached from the text:

"Unto you it is given to know the mysteries of the kingdom of God: but to others in parables; that seeing they might not see, and hearing they might not understand." (Luke 8 : 10.)

Sunday Afternoon.

The weather having cleared up, the congregation was much larger than in the morning.

Mr. Weaver preached an excellent discourse from the following text:

"Having the understanding darkened, being alienated from the life of God through the ignorance that is in them, because of the blindness of their hearts." (Ephes. 4 : 18.)

Sunday, October 22, 1854.

We have nearly reached the end of our labors. The church being now placed in a permanent location, and a regular minister being appointed, I shall introduce here the words of Solomon on the dedication of his temple:

"O Lord, my God! hearken unto the cry before thee to-day: that thine eyes may be open toward this house night and day, even toward which thou hast said, My name shall be there: that thou mayest hearken unto the prayer which thy servant shall make toward this place."

The Rector's sermon in the morning was from the following text:

"The same came to Jesus by night and

said unto him, Rabbi, we know that thou art a teacher come from God: for no man can do these miracles that thou doest except God be with him." (John 3 : 2.)

In the afternoon we assembled again, and, I trust, felt thankful to Providence, who seemed to address us in these words from the Book of Kings:

"I have surely built thee an house to dwell in, a settled place for thee to abide in for ever." (1 Kings 8 : 13.)

The Rector gave a very instructive discourse from the following text:

"Their webs shall not become garments, neither shall they cover themselves with their works: their works are works of iniquity, and the act of violence is in their hands." (Isaiah 59 : 6.)

When we consider the many difficulties—now overcome—in raising this humble structure for the worshippers of the "*Great Ruler of all*," we confess we experience no small satisfaction at taking part in the undertaking. It might appear invidious, when all were equally desirous of promoting the good work, to distinguish one above another, fully aware "*if the Lord built not the house, their labor is but lost that built it.*"

The feelings experienced by all on witnessing the completion of the enterprise, so long in hand, are expressed in the following lines:

Father of all, whose power alone
  Could raise this wondrous frame,
Where countless worlds your empire own,
  And magnify thy name,
How can we dare approach thy throne,
  The creatures of a day,
We to existence scarcely known,
  Ere fleetly passed away.

Lo! in the wilderness we raise
  A temple, Lord, to thee,
And celebrate thy glorious praise
  In sacred melody.
Then graciously thy Spirit pour
  Its influence around,
And fill the fane where we adore,
  To make it holy ground.

And when this transient life is o'er,
  (At best a short-lived flower,)
Its pleasures past, its griefs no more
  Extend their baneful power,

Oh! may we bless the day we cast,
In the Bethesda here,
The wound that had a power to last
Beyond this earthly sphere.

From the establishment of "*our Parish*" to the publication of these *Memorials*, a space of ten years has elapsed, of which we cannot say much, as we have resided but little there. During nine years Mr. Weaver discharged the duties of his responsible office to the satisfaction of the greater part of the parishioners, when, in consequence of the death of his truly excellent lady, he resigned his charge, and was succeeded by the Rev. Dr. Richey. We cannot omit this opportunity, as none other may occur, of expressing our gratitude for the many acts of kindness we experienced at the hands of the late incumbents of the "*Parsonage*." The death of Dr. Cammann was another affliction the parish endured previously. The character of Dr. Cammann is so fully given in the resolutions passed by two bodies with which he was connected, that further comment is unnecessary.

"The Managers of the Orphans' Home and Asylum of the Protestant Episcopal Church in New-York, on the occasion of the death of George P. Cammann, M.D., for a long period the Consulting Physician of the Home, deem it their duty, as it is their privilege, to place upon record their high sense of the many virtues which adorned his character, and their sorrow at the great loss which they and the little ones under their care have sustained in his death.

"Dr. Cammann held the office of Consulting Physician of the Orphans' Home for the space of eight years. During this period he visited the institution regularly, and was most assiduous and faithful in the discharge of his duties. It was to him a work of love, engaged in, as the Managers cannot but feel assured, from a conviction of Christian duty, and a desire to tread in the footsteps of Him who, when on earth, took up little children in his arms and blessed them. Like his Divine Master, he was kind, gentle, and compassionate, not only doing his work with skill and ability, but also with great tenderness and forbearance. Well did he deserve the title of the '*Beloved Physician*,' and as such will his memory long be cherished by the Managers and inmates of the *Orphans' Home*. He thought not of reward for all his toil. He looked not for the applause of men. But the Board rejoice in the hope that, resting now from his earthly labors, his works do follow him; that his reward is great in heaven; and that to him the Judge of all will, on the great day, address the cheering words: 'Well done, good and faithful servant, enter thou into the joy of thy Lord.'

"NEW-YORK, April 10, 1863."

At a meeting of the Vestry of St. James's Church, Fordham, held February twentieth, 1863, to take action in reference to the death of Dr. G. P. Cammann, one of the founders of this Parish, and for some years a Vestryman, the following preamble and resolutions were unanimously adopted:

IN MEMORIAM.

Whereas, It hath pleased Almighty God, in the wise dispensation of His Providence, to remove from this scene of labor and trial to one of rest and peace, our beloved friend and late associate, Doctor George P. Cammann.

Resolved, That in the death of Dr. Cammann we recognize the loss of a firm friend, a wise counsellor, and a liberal supporter of our parish, of which he was one of the founders, and for some years a member of the Vestry.

Resolved, That we record with thankfulness our high estimate of the healthy and Christian influence exercised in our midst by his consistent life and conversation, and in the remembrance of his pure example we find great reason to say with the wise King of Israel: "The memory of the Lord is blessed."

Resolved, That we are deeply conscious of the great and serious loss sustained to science in this removal of one occupying in his profession, so leading and prominent a position, and we sadly unite in regret and sympathy with a large class of our afflicted parishioners.

Resolved, That a copy of these resolutions be forwarded to the afflicted family of the deceased.

G. Ludlow Dashwood,
Clerk of the Vestry.

INDEX TO HUGUENOTS OF WESTCHESTER.

INDEX TO PARISH OF FORDHAM.

www.ingramcontent.com/pod-product-compliance
Lightning Source LLC
LaVergne TN
LVHW021421110826
845150LV00007B/2028

* 9 7 8 1 4 2 5 5 0 8 6 0 9 *